I Wish I Was A SEAGULL

Carmen Day

ISBN 978-1-64515-838-7 (paperback)
ISBN 978-1-64515-839-4 (digital)

Copyright © 2019 by Carmen Day

All rights reserved. No part of this publication may be reproduced, distributed, or transmitted in any form or by any means, including photocopying, recording, or other electronic or mechanical methods without the prior written permission of the publisher. For permission requests, solicit the publisher via the address below.

Christian Faith Publishing, Inc.
832 Park Avenue
Meadville, PA 16335
www.christianfaithpublishing.com

Printed in the United States of America

To my Lord and Savior for inspiring me
to write this book, also for blessing me with my wonderful family—
I love them very much. I pray that millions of parents enjoy reading
this book to their children. I look forward to writing more
children's books in the future.

I wish I was a seagull.
I would fly over the lake…

And fly…

And fly.

I would dive in the water to eat…

And eat…

And eat.

I would dive in the water…

And dive…

And dive.

I would walk on the sandy beach…

and walk…

And walk…

And walk.

If I was a seagull, I would stand on any surface…

and stand…

And stand.

If I was a seagull, I would hang out with other seagulls…

And hang…

And hang.

If I was a seagull, I would sit and watch what's going on around me…

And watch…

And watch…

And watch.

Why would I do
all these things?

Because if I was a seagull,
this is what seagulls
like to do, and this is
why I wish I was one!

All about seagulls.

A seagull is a medium-
to large-sized bird.
Usually white or gray
seagulls have long bills
and webbed feet.

Seagulls like to eat
small fish, marine worms,
grubs, spiders,
human food,
and…
anything you give them!

About the Author

My name is Carmen Day I am an Author and an artist. I use to have my own basket business called (Buddy Baskets) and I also went to college for business management, I graduated with great grades. I look forward to writing another children's book in the future for families to read together. When I was a child I enjoyed being read to please enjoy.